Law

of

Integration

by Mark F. Kailing, PsyD

Law of Integration

First published in 2016 by LaDena Kailing,
Copyright © 2016.

ISBN-13: 978-1530270613

ISBN-10: 1530270618

"This book is dedicated to my fellow philosophers, from whom humanity has been continually tutored. Much of my contribution is simply integrating their astounding discoveries. I also salute those precious few who continually seek truth no matter the cost—your courage gives humanity dignity and purpose, as well as hope."

-Dr. Mark Kailing

Imagine you are sitting in a small lecture room listening to profound ideas about human nature and how to effectively strengthen every area of your life. These deep topics are taught in an environment of love and concern for you. They are explained so simply that you are able to come to your own conclusion about each subject quickly. That is what the Self Mastery Lecture Series is.

This book is one of several from the Self Mastery Lecture Series, transcribed from recordings taken in 2011. Mark Kailing battled cancer during that time, but continued his weekly lectures. Dr. Kailing was a Psychologist for 16 years serving clients in California, Nevada and Utah.

He loved to teach. During his education a professor taught him, "You don't truly understand something until you can explain it simply". This led Mark to develop simplified theories on life, personality, the Universe, truth, core fears and more. His ability to make the profound simple is what made him a great teacher and leader. Dr. Kailing lectured to thousands of students and clients over the years. His self-mastery lecture series was one of his greatest accomplishments. He always lectured with a big smile on his face and spark in his eye. He was inspired by those who also desired to grow and improve in life.

Dr. Kailing passed away on May 21, 2013 after battling cancer for three and a half years. His example and influence have been felt by countless family, friends, clients, and colleagues. At the time of his death, he and LaDena had been married for 21 years and were raising their five children, Andrew (16), Aubrielle (15), Ammoriah (12), Ava (8) and Amari (4) in a home filled with adventures and love.

Einstein, about 60 years ago, stated; "Our technology has greatly outgrown our maturity."

That is a recipe for disaster in my opinion. That was many years ago, what has happened since then? Has our maturity greatly increased? Has our technology greatly increased? Our technology certainly has. We have a great growth in our technology but not the same in our maturity. Some even state that our maturity level has dropped. Einstein was terrified of this fact sixty years ago I wonder how he would feel about it now. He might greatly regret helping us by splitting the atom. He was regretting it back in his day.

A similar time in history happened to the ancient Greeks. Those existing around the Bronze Age, discovered how to make bronze for better metal, harder weapons, better plows and other tools. The technology of the ancient Greeks greatly expanded and they conquered the Mediterranean. Their maturity did not grow to keep up with their technology. They started arguing among themselves; there was always a threat of civil war. Things started to fall apart about half-way through their civilization. They were just not mature enough to handle that level of responsibility of having a great empire. Their civilization was about to break up before they did anything very impressive, but along came a philosopher, Socrates. Following up after him were his disciples Plato and Aristotle.

Socrates saved the Greek world. He came up with a philosophy that greatly increased the pace of their maturity. Their maturity was able to catch up with their technology. What happened is that this bought the Greeks a few centuries of prosperity. They became one of the wisest civilizations in history up to that point. We still have many ideas that affect us today. They were so advanced in their thinking.

All of this was accomplished with a philosophy. The philosophy stated that things are not totally up to the Gods. It isn't a random whim of the Gods, "Should we destroy the earth today? I don't know, let's flip a coin". Socrates taught that everything is run by logic. Everything in the Universe happens according to logical laws.

Human beings can understand the logic if we just think about it long enough. Imagine how popular that idea was. If we think hard enough we can understand the minds of the God. We can think like the Gods. It became very popular. Everyone wanted to become a philosopher. Kids were eager to learn in philosophy school. Socrates would stand at the corner market and people would bring him grapes and figs so they could listen to him speak. This greatly matured their society because it became popular. Not only was the philosophy magnificent, but it was cool, fun and exciting.

Could something like that save our society today?

We are on the edge of possible destruction of our civilization. We have all kinds of ways that we can destroy the world, we have all kinds of ways that we can destroy each other. Basically, every human being's life on the planet rests on one button controlled by the President of the United States. One button is all it takes.

I think that we need as much maturity as we can get. We need to get it fast. Could a philosophy save our modern world? Could it rapidly catch our maturity up to our technology? I believe I have come up with that philosophy. It's a bold, brass, arrogant thing to say and before I dared say it I tested it out for ten years on thousands of subjects.

This is a very important philosophy that I'm going to reveal to you today. It has the potential to save our civilization just as Socrates saved his.

The philosophy is not only a brilliant philosophy, but I think it's cool too. I think it might make people want to become philosophers. I've been practicing it on my patients for ten years and it has had overwhelming success, people are really excited about it. It has been the most successful psychological theory I have ever seen. As a psychologist I wanted to be broadly trained, so I studied all the different philosophies in psychology and they are magnificent. In my opinion, this one beats them all. I believe it has the most potential.

Before I reveal what this philosophy is, let's take a look at the modern world to see what this philosophy would need to achieve in order to solve our current problems.

One of the biggest problems of the modern world, that we talked about earlier, is maturity.

We are running out of time so it better be a philosophy that can mature us quickly. We need to grow decades, inside of a few years, if not faster.

Another big problem of modern society is laziness.

People don't want to work that hard. Now days we just push a button and things happen. Who would really want to commit to studying all the philosophies of the world and then practice what they have learned from all the world religions? Throughout history, for you to discipline your mind and really cultivate your mind would take a lifetime. It would take decades of study in college and following the masters. It is a very long process. Most people don't want to do that. We need a philosophy that will quicken the process and make it simpler.

Modern Americans just don't have the tolerance that we used to. We need things to be easy. Used to be, if you wanted to write a book, you would get out your stone tablet and chisel. Imagine writing a book like that! Now days we can accomplish big things fast. We need things to be fast in order to overcome our laziness.

Another big problem with humans is that we are afraid of truth.

I don't think we really want to know some of the answers in life. They are too scary. So, hopefully, we come up with a theory that makes the truth not so scary. It takes the sting out of every scary truth out there, otherwise human beings will avoid it. We avoid things that are scary. A huge problem with our modern society is that we are so divided. I wouldn't be surprised if there were a civil war in the next ten years right here in America. Our politicians, Republicans and Democrats dislike each other that much.

We have little in common with the different regions of America. We have more liberal coastlines and more conservative heartlands and it is difficult with all of the divided feelings that we have. I don't think that we feel that unity anymore. We don't have a love for each other like we're one big family. We go our separate ways and have our own philosophies then we pick on the other people who don't share our philosophies.

Hopefully this theory can solve all of that and unify everybody. It can lead us to see beauty in every philosophy. It can help us overcome all of this fear and mistrust so that we can just assume that all of these philosophies are beautiful. If someone wants to teach us something about their philosophy we'll think "Wonderful! I bet it's beautiful! I'd love to hear it!" instead of "Get away you weirdo!".

Another huge problem with our modern culture is that truth has become so complex.

I think it turns people off. Knowledge is coming at us so quickly that it's overwhelming. We become numb. How many people really want to watch the news anymore? It used to be our parents raced home from work, because they were bored out of their minds at work, so they could watch the news. They needed intellectual stimulation. They couldn't wait. Now, we come home and we are so overwhelmed and frazzled that we turn on The Simpsons. Watching the news would be too much.

The human mind can only take so much strain. The speed at which stimulation enters our mind is truly overwhelming. Not surprisingly, all of the stress-related illnesses such as; addiction, ulcers, headaches, suicidality, depression, fatigue are all rapidly on the rise reaching epidemic levels. Almost everybody has a stress-related illness nowadays. We keep throwing pills at it and then we just develop another stress-related illness on top of that one, and that one, and that one. The human mind is kind of like a Tetris video game.

Have you ever seen that video game Tetris? For those of you who haven't there are all of these geometric shapes coming down the screen and you have to rotate them by pushing the buttons on your computer. You have to rotate these shapes so that by the time they come down to the base of your screen they fit in an organized way. If they fit in an organized way, they dissolve and then your base will stay clear and easy to manage. If you don't rotate them well, if you let them randomly fall, your base doesn't dissolve and become clear. Pretty soon your screen is flooded with shapes and then it's 'game over'.

The human mind is like that. Truths come at us. Experiences come at us. Usually they come slowly, but they are always coming. We have to analyze them. We think, "What's that about? Why is Billy doing that? Why is that relationship like that? Why is Sally talking like that?" We have to analyze everything. If you analyze your experiences in an intelligent, organized way then your mind stays clear. You come up with a realistic perspective about some truth that is coming at you. Your mind is not distressed.

Reality is very comforting. If you have a realistic perspective, your mind is clear and comfortable. If you make errors in judgment instead, and look at things in an unrealistic way, you mind still has to think about it. It doesn't feel quite right. It doesn't quite fit. Your rationale won't be working for you. Then pretty soon, you'll have all these old things you've been working on for days, weeks, and years cluttering your mind.

Pretty soon your mind is just a fragile mess. You don't dare spend much time in your own head because it's uncomfortable up there. We start throwing pills and alcohol in there to quiet the noise in our head. Pretty soon it's 'game over'. We are not ourselves anymore. We are just robots walking around half mentally checked-out.

We have to come up with a theory that simplifies the truth. It very quickly gets the most realistic perspective on a situation. If you have a relationship problem with your boyfriend, girlfriend or spouse, you don't want to spend weeks on the issue because by then twenty other issues have come up. Hopefully you can look at that issue and within five minutes you can figure out exactly what's going on, get a very realistic, clear perspective on the issue and then you don't have to keep thinking about it. We need a theory that can simplify every problem imaginable. For every truth out there, it makes simple, quick sense out of it. That is very difficult to do. We are dealing with some major, complex issues.

Our best and our brightest in the modern day cannot agree on anything. Our politicians are fighting like kindergarteners on the playground over a cookie. If some intelligent civilization from another planet came and visited Earth and happened to set down in a session of Congress, they would quickly beam out and say, "This planet is not ready for first contact." They would bail on us. They would not find us impressive at all. If those are our best and our brightest, we have to do better. The problem is we are developing more and more complex issues;

assisted suicide, gay marriage, our economy is very complex, and the list goes on and on. These are issues that our best and our brightest will argue until they are blue in the face. They can't figure it out.

We need a theory that will handle all of this. It sounds impossible, right?

If you were a betting person you would say, there is no magic philosophy, no magic wand that is going to solve all of that. I think there is. It is a simple philosophy. It takes some practice to get used to it because frankly, it's like nothing we've ever been taught. Society has never really considered it before. It's built on looking at everything in life on a higher level. It is a universal theory that fits everything, and I mean everything. By the way, our scientists have tried to find a universal theory on everything and every time they thought they found it they were proven wrong. It sounds impossible for this to be the first universal theory of everything. You be the judge.

Remember I said that this theory needs to be profoundly simple, or people won't use it. Here is what we thought might be impossible, tell me if this sounds simple enough, here is that theory in one sentence;

We live in a universe where the most dominant law is that everything has an opposite and those opposites have to exist in equal balance.

That's it. Everything has an opposite, and those opposites need to exist in equal balance. There is no exception. Nothing in this universe can exist if it does not obey this law. How practical is that? How do we apply it in our daily lives? It sounds interesting but how do we apply it? Let's see how this could help the law of physics. The study of physics may be what has helped humanity the most throughout history. How much quicker would we have learned about physics if we knew this simple law of opposites long ago?

Sir Isaac Newton, all those years ago, came up with the theory that gravity exists. Centuries later we have discovered that anti-gravity exists. If Sir Isaac Newton knew that the law of opposites exists, as soon as he discovered gravity he would've said, "I'm sure anti-gravity exists somewhere." He could have assumed it without the use of any super microscopes that we have today that can prove it. He wouldn't need it. He could just sit back and trust. Scientists discovered matter and could trust that anti-matter exists. We've discovered time and we can trust that anti-time exists. There are theories that suggest that time is not a universal law, in some dimensions time does not exist. Time is relative, as

Einstein proved. If time exists, anti-time must exist also.

I've studied the top, thirty or so, principles of physics and if you look long and hard enough you'll find opposite principles existing also. Our modern scientists are finding opposites to every law we previously thought was universal. The reason this law of opposites can be the first universal theory is because it predicts that everything will have a contradiction. How do you contradict a theory that predicts that the theory will be contradicted?

One of the laws of thermodynamics is that every action has an equal and opposite reaction. At times in history we have used this law of opposites but we didn't fully know what to do with it. We didn't know how universal it was. Many people have pondered the idea of opposites. Haven't you ever had that thought? There is night and day, summer and winter, good guys and bad guys, but most people haven't thought of how universal this is.

This theory will greatly help in understanding physics, but how will this law help our society?

It basically says that you have to balance. The goal is to be realistic in our thoughts and actions so we can be happier. When you go against reality it hurts, right? So, to live our lives in a realistic way, all we have to do is to balance opposite parts of our lives. Don't become a workaholic who never gets to play. You need to balance your work with your play. Don't become a 'playaholic'. You have to balance your play with your work.

Apply this to daily living. Hopefully you're resting as much as you're exerting energy. Hopefully you're spending as much time in isolation as you are socializing. You don't want too much of one or the other, it's not realistic. You have to keep these things in balance. This theory tells us how to live our lives in the most realistic way.

Most psychological problems that I work with in my office, I'll just pay attention to what side of life they are missing. If you are doing too much of something, I encourage them to try some of the opposite. This can affect us not just individually but as a society.

One of the subjects I like to study is politics as well as history. I'm convinced that our government would be far better off if they had just balanced opposites throughout history. For whatever political issue that came across the President's desk, what if he had chosen to balance both sides and do something in the middle, something moderate, every single time for the past two hundred years? I believe our country would be far better off. I don't think we can imagine how better off we would be.

All the complex political problems of our modern world that are tearing us apart and causing us to hate one another, I think if we did something down the middle on each one of them we would be in a more realistic realm. We'd be in a situation far better than following the extremists that want it totally their way and the extremists who want it totally the opposite way. Extremists generate hate. Extremists generate paranoia. They are living an unrealistic life. They are only seeing half of the issue.

When we do something extreme it begets opposite extremes. People say, "Drastic times call for drastic measures" and that would be the temptation, but every action has an equal and opposite reaction. When we bomb a country, we generate a lot of hatred for our country. When we dropped an atomic bomb we generated a lot of hate for our country. They didn't drop an atomic bomb in return, but they dropped a psychological bomb, a spiritual energy bomb of hatred. When someone hates you, you feel that, and it sickens you, it weakens you. The United States has much of the world hating them. I don't want to go through life with one person hating me, I can feel that and I don't feel good. With that much hatred at our country it will lead to sickness.

When someone does something extreme the temptation is to do something extreme in reaction because it serves as a temporary fix but then you end up paying for it down the road. Sometimes the consequences are not immediate. The consequences are sometimes gradual, somewhere down the road. So, we have to resist the temptation to have a quick fix that may help things for today, but doesn't pay off in the long run.

Sometimes I call this law of opposites 'Pendulum Theory'.

When something gets pulled to one extreme, you just can't bring it back to the middle immediately. It has to swing to the opposite side. It has to. Sometimes what we have to do is a little bit of the opposite extreme, for a little while just to relieve some of the pressure. Let me give you an example; sometimes I'll have a woman come in for counseling and say that she has been a victim for ten years and that she has been abused and victimized in a relationship. She's passive, too eager to please and takes care of everybody else besides herself. I don't tell her to be moderate right away, not instantly. I tell her that you have to do the opposite extreme for a little while. You've got to go and be alone for a while, you have to focus on yourself for a while and get a little angry for a while. Often times these women will go through these stages including an angry stage where they are fighting back before settling into the middle. Sometimes they will stay stuck on the victim side, and sometimes they will be stuck on the angry side. I tell them, "Go ahead and go to the angry side, but keep in mind that the middle is where you need to be eventually. The angry side is a temporary luxury that you are allowing yourself and as soon as you can we've got to moderate that."

Another example is America and our current economy, overspending has ruined our economy. Perhaps we need to go through a period of being extra-careful with our spending, just to let the pendulum swing to the opposite side for a while before it settles somewhere in the middle. I don't think it's enough to just start moderating our spending right away. We were too far left, now we have to go too far right for a little while. We might have to go through an extended period of ten, twenty or thirty years of Americans going without things. Americans learning to go without the luxuries they are used to, to pay for all of the times we had goodies handed out to us that we couldn't afford. When you borrow a bunch of money, don't you expect to go without some things for a long time before it's paid off? Our country has to do the same thing. Let's apply this theory to other aspects of life.

Let's apply this theory to truth itself.

This theory is saying that everything has an opposite. That means that every truth has an opposite truth. This is a mind-boggling proposition and to be honest with you this is what took me these ten years. I thought, "That *can't* be", but after ten years I haven't found a truth that didn't have an opposite truth.

You have to look for it sometimes. It's hard to find but it's there. Our entire civilization has been based off the idea that only one side can be true. Our scientists are looking for one side of the truth, not multiple sides of the truth. Our entire scientific method is to search for the one truth. Our court system is looking for the one person who is guilty in the room. If you were to look closely, every person in the room is guilty. We all have some guilt, we're human, right? So, we all have some guilt. Our society has thought in this black or white way that one side is true and one side is false. It's kind of how a child thinks.

Psychologist Piaget, you might have heard of him, studied how intelligence evolves from childhood to adult. He used that term, 'black or white thinking' as a way to describe the thinking of a child. A child can only think in black or white terms.

Ask a kid, "Is that a good guy or a bad guy?" They don't say, "He's kinda good and kinda bad. He is both." They get confused when a guy in a white hat does something bad because good guys are always good and bad guys are always bad. They get confused when Mommy or Daddy blows their temper. They think, "They are supposed to be good. My world doesn't make sense anymore."

In our teenage years we develop the ability to think in terms of shades of grey in a more realistic view. Everything is a mixture of everything. Everyone has both good and bad in them at the same time. Things are both fair and unfair at the same time. Things are in shades of grey, somewhere in the middle. Since we've evolved and have the ability to see things more realistically doesn't mean we always do. When we get lazy we give up our ability, we don't use our ability. It's much easier to think in terms of black or white. When we get scared, black or white thinking is a great defense against our insecurities. If I'm insecure, all I have to do is tell myself, "I'm great and everybody else sucks." Black and white thinking is easy, and it helps us hide from the scary truth.

All we have to do is to write that scary truth off as there is nothing valid about it. Our friends try and cheer us up using this black or white thinking. When a boyfriend dumps you, your friends will say,

"Oh, he's just a jerk, you're so wonderful! Everyone would be lucky to go out with you. He is the one with the problem." They feed us black or white thinking because it's comfortable, and I hate to tell you this but it's only half true.

Truth is in the middle.

Psychologists have been bad at this too. If you go to a Psychologist with a fear, the Psychologist will try and tell you that the fear is not true. A paranoid person believes that someone is out to get them and the psychologist will tell them, "No one is out to get you." The reality is there are people all over the world who are out to get us. Terrorists, right now, are out there trying to destroy us. There are meetings happening in back rooms, right now, plotting against us.

When people come in with a fear, I will try and teach them that the fear is half true, that is a little more comforting that it being totally true. So I at least half comfort the patient. To be honest with you, we should only be half comforted. If you're too comfortable in life, you aren't learning. I became a lot happier in life once I accepted this fact. I had been trying to be perfectly comfortable, getting all of the comforts I thought I needed so I could get my life to be totally happy. I gave up on that fantasy for a more realistic perspective, that life is supposed to be half happy, and half miserable. That is how you learn is when you are moderately uncomfortable.

Psychology has discovered through research that people learn best under moderate pressure and moderate discomfort. When we are too comfortable we are lazy. When we are too uncomfortable our mind narrows, we have paranoia and get defensive.

Moderate pressure is the best situation for learning.

Once I accepted that moderate pressure was the best way to be, the best thing for me and that God or nature had intended it to be so and that was what was necessary for my long-term, eternal life, I was glad for it. If the day was moderately kicking me in the butt I would say, "Good!" We always get crushed in our marriages because our spouse is only half of what we want. We don't have this Disney marriage where the spouse is everything in the universe and has every human trait developed, and offers every gift to you on a silver platter.

Disney has done us a disservice. That is not reality. Your spouse will half comfort you and half torment you and that's perfect. That's perfect. Count yourself lucky. What hurts in a marriage is that our spouse is exposing truths that are uncomfortable truths. You cannot be a whole human being until you accept all the uncomfortable truths as well as the comfortable truths. When somebody is pissing us off they are doing us a great favor. The reason we are angry is that there is some truth there that we don't like. You could choose to hide from the truth for the rest of your life and never be fully healed and whole and realistic, or you can accept that painful truth. At least accept that truth in moderation as half true. Then you are free.

Fear is basically self-inflicted.

We fear things because we think in black or white terms we think, "I'm afraid of this thought because if it were totally, 100% true, it would be terrifying". What are the things we fear, death? If I were to believe I would be totally dead, never to live again in heaven, that would be totally terrifying, but death is only half-true. We half die. Our bodies die. Our spirits still exist. So, death is only half true. That's not so scary, is it? If somebody says you're going to die, totally, 100% forever right now, that would be terrifying. If somebody said you're going to only half die, that's not so bad.

Does this law apply in heaven?

This law of opposites only pertains to this universe, this physical, plane of existence that we are all on. Heaven is not a place of half pleasure, half pain, half good and half evil. This physical dimension is meant for a training universe, where souls go to get trained and it must have opposites. You need a moderate amount of challenges.

Let's say you are a boxer and you are in a boxing match with someone that is way better than you, would you learn much? Probably not, you might be knocked out in three seconds and wouldn't remember any of it. What if you were in a boxing match with someone way inferior to you? You wouldn't learn anything, you might read a book while you were knocking him around. When you're in the ring with someone who is an equal match to you, you learn the most. God and nature being so wise, we live in a dimension where these opposites are equally matched, paired against each other.

Every truth has an opposite truth, this contradicts everything we've ever learned. You have to really stretch your mind. If you are willing to stretch your mind and consider the opposite truth you will come up with ideas that no human being has ever thought of. I've challenged many students to come up with a philosophy, and idea, that I can't find some truth in.

One time the class thought they had me. There was a candy wrapper on the floor and they said "That candy wrapper is the queen of England". Well, let's see, a wrapper is like a title, it has a title around it and the Queen is really just a title, a wrapper that she wears. If you look at it on the molecular level, human beings are all made up from recycled carbon atoms on this planet. That wrapper is just recycled atoms into a different form. You can argue this from the eastern philosophy, which is brilliant, which is that everything in this universe is one sea of energy. There is no separation between objects and everything in the universe is one life form. Energies flow right through you, me, the air, the earth, and separation is an illusion. Separation is a dumbed-down version of the truth. So, that candy wrapper IS the Queen of England. If you are willing to be the only human being on the planet who will argue the opposite side you will come up with new discoveries that others have not thought of.

It will take breaking a very bad habit because all of your training thus far has been to find the one truth. We've been taught that if something sounds stupid, it can't be true.

There is some truth in everything.

I would go so far as to say that a human being cannot have a thought that does not have some truth in it. Everything is made of spiritual energy and spiritual energy is basically truth. Everything is made of these truths, even your thoughts. If anything exists, it is made of truths. Your thoughts exist, therefore they are made of truths.

Now, truths can be combined incorrectly, like when people use the phrase "when pigs fly". Pigs exist and flying exists, but those two concepts are just combined incorrectly. Pigs don't fly. Like that, our thoughts might be combined incorrectly, little pieces of truth combined incorrectly like if a carpenter takes a bunch of little, different boards and builds the house wrong. The house is still built with good lumber, just like a false statement is built on a bunch of little truths that were combined incorrectly. In any argument you can find valuable truths. If a house is built incorrectly, you don't just burn the house down. You take apart the good lumber and reuse pieces of it. It's the same thing when someone comes up with a false argument, don't throw the whole thing out. Don't burn the argument down. Find the valuable gems in it. You will be a person who gleans a lot of valuable knowledge along the way. Most people just say, "That's dumb. That's dumb. That's dumb", and dismiss a lot of things. Like our teenagers in junior high who say, "That sucks. That sucks. That sucks, but hey that one is cool." Ninety percent of the things they study, they will say 'it sucks' and once they think it sucks do they learn anything from it? They close off a bunch of knowledge. We shouldn't consider any argument as totally wrong or totally sucking. There are nuggets of truth in there.

What if there was a big pile of manure here but there was a diamond somewhere in it?

Wouldn't you sift through all that manure, by hand to find that diamond? Sure we would. It is a valuable diamond. I'd sift through that manure, and worse. It's the same thing with truth. Don't pass up all these piles of manure because there are little diamonds in all of them. Diamonds are found in the coal. Gold is found in the dirt.

Let's give a challenging argument, say someone came up to me and said, "Dr. Kailing you're a jerk! You suck!" Our natural, human instinct would be a fear that the argument is totally true. If that statement were totally true, it would be scary, so the temptation is to be defensive, "No, you totally suck and I'm totally good." Then, I've just missed a golden opportunity to learn a lot of things. What I need to do when someone says I totally suck is to sift through some of that manure. I know I don't *totally* suck, let's see if there is any valuable knowledge in there. So I'd ask why do they think I suck, is it because I'm often late? Well that's a diamond, I'd better take that one to heart. I kind of suck because I'm an airhead and I don't catch everything? I don't remember my children's birthdays? There are many other numbers of diamonds that I could learn from. There are all kinds of things that I could learn in there if I'm not afraid of that truth; that in some ways I suck.

In some ways we all suck. If you want to be enlightened you have to accept that fact. To make this earth life incredibly educational for you, God or nature had to create an equal match of good and suckiness. So He made you half good and half to suck. It wouldn't be a fair match otherwise, would it?

It wouldn't be a great test for you either if God made you perfectly wonderful in every way. Gosh, you'd have nothing to learn. You'd have no weaknesses to wrestle with. What a wasted life that is.

How does this theory apply to love?

There are so many different types of love, but we could say that the opposite of love is hate. There are some things in this life we should hate. Let's talk about marriage for a minute. When people first get married, they think they need to totally love everything about their spouse and they are crushed when they discover things they don't love about their spouse. There will be things about your spouse that you hate, that's natural. There are things you love about your spouse and things you hate about your spouse. Some days your spouse will be acting out the things you love about them, other days they will act out the things you hate about them. So, when people say, "I still love you, even though I'm mad at you and yelling at you", I say, "Hogwash, you hate them right now, and that's okay". What's so scary about that?

To me, this pressure to always have to love our children, to always have to love our spouses, to always have to be in love is unrealistic. We try to convince ourselves we are still in love while we are yelling. No you're not, you're hating. I know the difference between love energy and hate energy and that doesn't feel like love. It's okay to hate parts of your spouse. Love to some degree is an attachment and the opposite would be a detachment.

This describes Western and Eastern religions; the Eastern say detach and Western say "Love and attach to everybody". It's driven both religions a little nutty. You need to be moderate. You have to be moderately attached and moderately detached. You can't love somebody so much that you are off-balance about it. You could become obsessive, a fatal attraction kind of thing, or controlling and fearful. It is best to be moderately detached. I love the person, but I don't *need* them. I'm not desperate for them. Extreme love is an unhealthy thing; it means you can't be without the person.

A good marriage is described as a vine, sometimes growing together and sometimes experiencing independence.

Independence is a great lesson. Dependence is a great lesson. A good relationship has periods of both. A good vine becomes strong by going in and out of the other vine, so do we go in and out of each other's lives. A relationship that's too dependent is not very strong. If you do anything extreme in life there will be an equal and opposite reaction, so if you love somebody too hard will you eventually swing to the opposite side and hate them? The answer is yes. If you love somebody too much it will become unrealistic and painful you may go 'fatal attraction' on them and want to kill them.

We only have power in this world to do things moderately if you do something extreme it will be short-lived, it won't last and it will have an opposite pendulum swing undoing everything you have worked on. Things that grow at a slow and steady pace in life, tend to be around forever. They are stable. Things that grow real fast tend to collapse real quickly as well. Slow and steady like the mighty oak tree. Consider these opposite truths because they greatly expand the mind.

Let's take this law of opposites, because laws have to exist in equal balance, let's apply this to the personality.

Ultimately, the thing that matters most in life is that we develop our personality.

Our personality is the only thing that we take with us after this life. It matters who you really are inside. It's our work of art. It's our masterpiece. It's our only thing of eternal value. How do we create a perfect personality? That is where our energy should be, that's where our efforts should be in life. It doesn't matter if something is fair or unfair. Eternally that doesn't matter.

How did it affect my personality? How it affects your personality is really up to how you interpret the situation. How do we perfect the personality? No one has really known. It hasn't been made clear until this theory explains the issue. How valuable would it have been to know that our job is to perfect our personality, now, how do we do it? Nobody ever knew.

Take a look at how simple this becomes when we apply the law of opposites. Every personality trait has an opposite personality trait and you have to balance them in equal measure. How simple that is. How profoundly simple it is. It is sublime. If you are an assertive person, better not be extremely assertive or you will be in jail. What does that assertive person need to do? Balance their assertiveness with some passivity, then there will be a perfect balance of those two traits. Then, they will live a realistic, healthy life in this dimension, obeying the law of opposites that dominates this universe.

If you are a logical person, you'd better not be too logical like Mr. Spock or you will never get a date, not being able to relate well with others. The opposite of logical is emotional. We don't want to be too emotional either or people will run from you, they will date you for about five minutes and then they will run. Your perfect personality will balance your logic and your emotions, you'll have a little bit of both.

Are you a serious person or are you humorous? If you are an extremist on either end you won't get along well with people, you need to shoot for something in the middle. People like a moderate person. Sometimes we'll like the extremist for a little while, then they get irritating. Have you ever been at a party where someone was really funny? At first it's great and then after a while you grow tired of it, you wish they would dial it down a little bit and be more in the reality zone.

We found the secret to possibly the most important thing in your life, perfecting your personality.

Everything comes from your personality. Your relationships are basically a result of your personality. Your job, your wealth, your level of education, and your health are all a result of your personality. Your personality is the only thing you take with you and now you know how to simply work on it throughout your life. One of the dumb things that our society, culture, and even psychology has done, is to say, "Just be yourself", and "Follow your heart". That is only half true. That is only telling you the stuff that is easy. It doesn't really help you in the long run.

Who do you need to be? Half yourself, and half the opposite of yourself, so you can get balanced out. Whatever traits come naturally for you, you already know. Those are easy. It's the stuff you've already learned. It's important to keep learning. What is new in your growth? What are you learning lately? People who choose to just be themselves will just stay the same for the rest of their lives. That means you won't grow.

The idea of following your heart is not always good for you because your heart wants a lot of bad things. I think on some level we all want wine, women and song, as they say and if you follow your heart it will tell you to follow the easiest answer. Our heart is like a child, our mind is like a parent. Which one are you going to listen to? Do you always follow the advice of a child? We have to use our head and our heart. You don't always want to be a parent and not listen to the child's feelings either. That is no way to make decisions. A child has great power. A child can feel things sensitively, that a parent can't feel. A parent can learn from a child, but the child needs to learn from the parent too.

Whenever you have a decision to make, you balance your logic with your gut, your heart. Balance the two out. Let me give you some practical tips. We've been focused on a lot of philosophy today, let me share some practical advice that you can start using this week. The ideal state is to be moderate. If you are a moderate, you are a balance of both sides. You're not too far left or too far right, you are somewhere in the middle. You want to be moderate in everything; your personality, your beliefs, your behaviors.

It's important to ask yourself, what stands out about you?

What is the most extreme thing about you? That is the thing that will cause you pain eventually. Whatever stands out about you means it's extreme, it's not moderate. If it stands out, it's loud, it's obvious, it means you're off-balance on that thing.

It's unrealistic and will cause pain eventually. Sometimes you'll get away with it for a little while but eventually it causes pain. One reason that's true is because when we go too far to one side, we have to ask ourselves why we would want to do that. It takes a lot of our energy, why would we do it?

The reason is that the opposite side is something that we are afraid of. There is some terrifying thing on the opposite side that we are running from and we would rather live in all this strain and effort than to face that fear. So, whatever stands out about you, you can be sure you are afraid of the opposite. The opposite is a fear you've been hiding from. It's a truth that you've been ignoring and eventually life will require you to know that truth. You'll need to use that trait, and you don't have it, you're not going to fit that situation in life.

An aggressive person is actually afraid of being passive. Sooner or later they are put in a situation that will humble them. If they resist the situation it's because they haven't developed that personality trait. When you are too far in one direction, you will cause the other to happen eventually. We will cause our core fears to happen. Every action has an equal and opposite reaction so if you run to the right, you are eventually going to cause yourself to swing to the left. You will swing to the side you are afraid of. An aggressive person will eventually cause a situation where he has to be passive, even if he has to sit in jail in order to learn passivity.

"Be moderate", is a great rule of life. In order to do that, we will have to argue against ourselves. It is a great philosophical exercise. Whatever you believe, ask yourself why you don't believe the opposite side. If you're a Republican, ask yourself why you don't find some truth from the Democrats. Whatever your belief is you will find some truth in the opposite side too. The opposite side has some diamonds hidden in that manure. If you like Country music but not Rock and Roll, go find some diamonds there.

Once you start combining truths you'll find more opposites. There is always more to discover. You don't even want to be perfectly moderate. The balance requires moderation in all things, and what is the opposite of moderation but extremism. You need a balance of both. You can't be perfectly balanced constantly, sometimes you have to go to the left or go to the right, depending on the situation.

The balance in between extremism and moderation would be to swing just a little bit. On a scale of one to ten you don't want to jump from a one to a ten. You don't want to be a perfect five either.   You want to be a person who swings between a six and a four.   Remember that the farther you go to one extreme, you are just going to end up swinging to the opposite extreme.   The harder you work, the harder you'll sleep. When you are extreme too long, you will have to pay for it. Another really important aspect of balancing our lives is to split the blame with people.

One of the things we fear the most is blame.

That is when we really get extreme. When someone tries to blame us we fight back. We get into these childish black or white thinking. In any situation at all never think you are innocent. Never think you are totally innocent.   We are all moderately guilty and moderately innocent. When it comes to any argument it is partly true. There is some truth in it somewhere. For example, did we cause the starvation in Africa? Our instinct is to say, "No way, that is not true and I'll never consider that idea as truth!"

Let's be brave for a second and think about how we all had a little cause in it. What arguments could we come up with to support that? We will probably come up with some arguments that no one else has considered, let's take a look. One spiritual theory is that all the plants of the Earth respond to our spiritual purity as human beings.   When a civilization is pure and good, the weather is good, the plants grow more abundantly, animals don't hurt people as much, but we live in times when human beings are generating the worst energy, the most evil, angry, hateful energy. There tends to be a lot of wild things happen with weather, droughts, plants dying, animals are dying.

One spiritual philosophy is that the Earth is just responding to our spiritual purity.

If every human being on the Earth was spiritually evolved there would be a lot of food growing around us. There would be plenty of food for everybody. Is the weather in Africa affected by our purity? Yes, to a degree, maybe a small degree. Every bad thing on the planet is partly caused by our negativity, by our being spiritually unhealthy. We are all partly responsible for all of the mess. If everybody had a great spiritual purity I don't think we would suffer, not even death. I don't think there would be disease at all, if everyone had a high enough spiritual energy radiating around them.

It's an interesting theory. If you are willing to split the blame with people instead of going to black or white thinking, you stay humble and open to learning. You would be learning about the things that you fear. They are just doing you a favor exposing things you fear. You will become an enlightened, whole human being, just by being humble enough to split the blame, see the truth on both sides.

Typically you will make a friend out of an enemy when you practice this. You could stay an enemy, totally putting the blame on one another, and have all this hatred, or you can be humble and say, "I'm sure my weaknesses have contributed to this situation somehow, I'm sorry for my part in that."

You want to practice that kind of language saying, "I'm sorry for my part in that." Notice how I said, 'my part', I'm not saying it is all my fault. I'm not taking all of it. "I'm sure I'm partly at fault." When we use this language, we don't even need to argue and know all of the details. If we just get to the middle we'll be healthy.

One of the neat things about this theory, as I write about it I call it "The Perspective of Genius" because every person can be a genius with this theory. If you took all of the knowledge of the Universe, you would just conclude that the truth is in the middle. Every human being can say that the truth is somewhere in the middle, without knowing all the truth in the Universe they went to the same conclusion as someone who did study everything in the Universe.

If you just simply have faith in this and say, "I'm sure the truth is somewhere in the middle", you will have the perspective of a genius. It's a short cut. It's the answer sheet to the test. Develop the habit of saying these moderate statements; "I'm sure it's half my fault. I'm sorry for my part." and "I should've been more moderate on that, how about we split the difference and meet somewhere in the middle". We should develop this kind of language because it very quickly gets a situation to a very

The other books in Mark Kailing's Self-Mastery Lecture Series:

Purpose of Life

Dark Side of Relationships

Map of the Mind

The Gender War

Deeper Relationships

Battling our Core Fears

A Profoundly Open Mind

Lifelong Path of Grace

What We Now Know

Improve your Mental Health by Improving your Physical Health

Self-Mastery and Religion

Your Spiritual Path

Overcome Your Core Fears

www.ingramcontent.com/pod-product-compliance
Lightning Source LLC
Chambersburg PA
CBHW071259280526
45788CB00004B/1772